Portrait of a Young Girl Falling

Katrina Moinet

Wild | *Sauvages*

she
who's she / the cat's mother
another lover / of animal binaries
nature versus / reverse cowgirl
gender bent / on defining
boundaries / that no longer limit
selves / as sexual
preference / no longer simple
choice between / which toilet door
looks more appealing / rather
disarm language / burn the letter
of the law / pull up that drawbridge
between you / and me / and a she
i was told to be

in public places / private spaces
obtain domain names / suited to
this fresh young age / we live in
we love in / plurality
of minds / we think in
we

How to be both

pretty good, pretty sweet
pretty kind, pretty quiet
pretty cute, pretty neat
pretty smart, pretty polite

pretty messy, pretty sassy
pretty moody, pretty cheeky
pretty sexy, pretty sarky
pretty awkward, pretty easy

pretty tight, pretty loose
pretty S &, pretty M
pretty masturbator
pretty ejaculator

pretty seen-and-now-heard
pretty [insert]
pretty [insert personality]
pretty [insert own construct here]

Elemental | *Elémentaire*

Tell me all the ways you'll conquer me
> a gentle *chuchotement à l'oreille*
> a ramrod *battement* between my *enjambe-*
> *ment* sweet *châtiment ça chatouille* bare skin
> fingertip *frissons* tiptoe to seduce
> *la nuque*, misuse your *langue civilisée*
> to recite a *malaise* of easy beats
> to slipknot bind me *à l'horizontale*

I'll tell you the way I'll conquer you
> as hawthorn borne over by prevailing winds
> as loosened dune concedes to groundswell flood
> as a flame-scorched page disintegrates to
> nothing
>> but love, relentless love

US of A

after Gwendolyn Brooks

We real smart. We
School stars. We
Get laid. We
Bed made. We
Bled late. We
Wrong state. We
~~Erased too soon.~~

Unborn Lives

a cautionary tale-end / meets brief encounter
as we flounder between rock and / a hard placed
seed of doubt / sown before we'd grown
any place to sow warm oats / left cold inside

this solitary abyss to fall in / line
rote-learned choice / piety
earned by erasing past / empty
brain fuelling / relentless swelling

mind degrading / forced collaboration
fit-for-purpose nation / of chosen resources
skilled retorts that purport to know / my inner-most
thoughts till I blurt out *I'm keeping her!*

this life? / this unborn life? / this right
to a childhood before a child

Father's day

did not occur again today / is a blank
memory / rank cinematic snapshots
gathered in / yellowing albums
albumen-sealed / a lifetime under
cellophane / in order / to prevent
ground   shifting

forgive me father / for i have
shunned / your utter existence while
gripped by / catholic resistance
unashamedly i admit to / living a life
of free love / free speech / free from
any future   therapy

i've never been troubled by father's
day / or week / or month / or year

This is not a protest

your short-skirted verse makes me turn my head
such low-cut openings shouldn't be seen

those bare-legged end line rhymes parch my mind
thirst for attention to question intention

your playful form leads down dark-alleyed thoughts
such long-drawn vowels drown nubile consonants

cause affront to my eye, harden my ear
please tone down your volume!

why can't you just stick to masculine feet
speak the bard's measured iambic tight pent-

a meter should treat men with due respect
dress those stanzas down appropriately

you're responsible for the response you
arouse in the reader   aren't you?

Small Consequence

black lace lies on dirty white stilettos
  I don't mean that symbolically

recalling absent-mindedness
  I don't mean that casually

sensing a presence in the room
  I don't mean spiritually

my body unclothed eyes closed
  I don't mean metaphorically

waking naked, silent
  I don't mean figuratively

at peace with the world
  I don't mean allegorically

till I see   my underwear left   somewhere it's never been left
                    folded   my entire life

Out of Harm's Way

after Kim Moore

Is it self-harm
                    if I fell in harm's way
Is it self-neglect
                    if I don't care for my own welfare
Is it self-forgetting
                    if I took no time to heal
Is it self-soothing
                    if I suck on the memory
Is it self-loathing
                    if the memory sucks on me
Is it self-effacing
                    if I turn away from the mirror
Is it self-aware
                    if I trusted the universe to guide me
Is it a crime
                    if I let him rape me twice

The Art of Falling

What else is gravity but a constant
falling towards the earth's surface.
What is it to feel grounded when the earth
never fails to rise to meet you.

Today, I kept myself upright and whole.
Gravitational attraction
retracts the longer I stand in my soul
and stare at cracks in the ceiling.

What danger lies in feeling light-headed?
Pressure of weightlessness occurs
in freefall, as ground rushes up to kiss
me cold, and seizures pocket time.

It's never the fall that kills you, or else
it's killing me a fraction more each day.

La Petite Mort

O, *la petite mort*
mirror-flicker souls fixed in
frozen wordless O

little orgasm
death, blooms on ruddy cheeks beet-
rooted in bedsheets

sleeved in sweat and pale
air, galloping arteries
gasp oxygen hy-

poxia for two
parallel minds plundering
small mortal pleasure

Ω

Over in a flash
a seizure's sweet effacement
sudden abasement

vacant stare, synapse
snaps at atlas vertebra
star-stuffed ears hissing

—*it's here!* brain erased
death-drop embrace, contorting
as spectator sport

till Orpheus hooves me
back from sensory stasis
life rinsed— O, relief

after Sylvia Plath

15

City[e]scape

I'm a shifting face *insta*taneous race 2snap
chattering birds in trees & bees honeying
screens; outwardly calm reflections gather
4inner dawn chorus wake a city's porous
heart, attack social dominion, stack public
opinion, rouse dull minds to annotate
redundant 280-character lines

mediated thought drifts in & outside
dwelling spheres; socially distanced ear
lodged *en route*/commute back home door
slams shut, alone: a tiny bright bulb lights my
phone, hermetic seal broken, healing this
thisness empty nest pressure, filling days
with words and words and words

I May Destroy You

I consider the pros and cons   of consent
how sensual   consensual   must feel
done right   some former Mr Right   unreal
reality bites   a raw hand   once dealt
left asexual   irrevocable words
(buried) cacophony of recognition:

I'd danced my way into a corner to think
long and hard about what   I   had done

An unseen ring grows inside my tree
slim band of memory   tender dignity
needs tending to   too painful
to uproot   regrowth
cannot regenerate   that / self-
same security   erasure / so sure

Submission

Vivisection

I think of you daily, which is not to say fondly.

I'm waiting for that memory to return
the one that confirms you monster, and I
more vulnerable than I'd care to remember.

What is it to love a person who wronged you
other than a reconditioned love?

Disclosure implies a letting go / confession:
how was I to know I'd allocated you
a tiny square of my heart.
Dissection suggests some swift separation
cleanly halved and yet I've found it
far more jagged / less deliberate.

You know what they say, when one door closes
another trauma opens.

Remembrance: on the provenance of trauma

we were where we were where we were where we were
we were where we were where we were where we were
we were where we were where we were where we were
we were where we were where we were where we were
we were where we were where we were where we were
we were where we were where we were where we were
we were where we were where we were where we were
we were where we were where we were where we were
we were where we were where we were where we were
we were where we were where we were where we were
we were where we were where we were where we were
we were where we were where we were where we were
we were where we were where we were where we were
where we were where we were where we were we were

after Zoë Skoulding

Notes & Acknowledgements

With immense gratitude to Zoë Skoulding and Joey Frances for their guidance and encouragement during my Master's studies at Bangor University, and beyond. I am grateful to early readers of this work, and much love goes to my husband, daughter, friends, and family for all their incredible support.

With thanks to the editors of the journals where these poems first appeared: 'Wild | *Sauvages'* in *The Post Grad Journal,* issue 6; 'I May Destroy You' in *Firmament Vol. 2, No. 4*, 2022, Sublunary Editions, Seattle; 'Vivisection' in *The Poetry Marathon Anthology 2024.*

And finally thank you, Mark Davidson, for believing in my work.

1. 'US of A' came in the wake of the US Supreme Court 2022 decision to overturn the Roe vs. Wade ruling which had guaranteed women the right to abortion. This poem is inspired by 'We Real Cool' from Gwendolyn Brooks' 1960 collection *The Bean Eaters.*

2. 'This is not a protest' longlisted in Mslexia Poetry Competition 2022, judged by Pascale Petit, and originally responded to Helen Mort's 'Skirt' from the collection *No Map Could Show Them*, Random House, 2016.

3. 'Out of Harm's Way' responds to Kim Moore's poem 42, 'Is it ███', from the collection *All the Men I Never Married,* Seren, 2021.

4. 'City[e]scape' arose in workshop responses to Rimbaud's 'Ville' in *Les Illuminations*, 1875, and Sean Bonney's 2009 'abandonedbuildings' https://abandonedbuildings.blogspot.com/2009/08/after-rimbaud.html.

5. 'Remembrance: on the provenance of trauma' is inspired by Zoë Skoulding's 'A Short Presentation on the Current Direction of Travel' from *A Marginal Sea,* Carcanet, 2022.

"'Portrait of a Young Girl Falling' is the feminist poetry I want for my train journey, my bath, my coffee, and my life. Katrina is in control of her themes yet shows a sensitivity to the subjects within her poems, and this gives power. This is why I read poetry. We need poetry like this, unexpected as it is confident, hard at times, messy, bodily, but alive with women."

Wendy Allen, *Plastic Tubed Little Bird*

"From the outset, Katrina Moinet's debut collection pulls us into the world of the 'she/i was told to be' with honest and rich poems that explore feminine trauma and healing. We are led from the chilling 'Out of Harm's Way' through to the fighting 'Vivisection'. We can stand with the emerging 'pretty seen-and-now-heard', bear witness with the 'We' in the 'Wrong state' and listen to the 'I have a voice' that should be heard."

Ness Owen, *Moon Jellyfish Can Barely Swim*

"All too often, women exist in the negative space of language; we are defined by what we are not. Moinet, with her dexterous and remarkable poetry, captures this and revolts against language itself, unveiling the trauma that inevitably follows a life lived in patriarchal shadows. 'Portrait of a Young Girl Falling' is intense, visceral, and will leave its teeth in you for a long time after reading. It is a staggering accomplishment."

Briony Collins, *The Birds, The Rabbits, The Trees*

"If 'Portrait of a Young Girl Falling' looks back on the vulnerability that its title suggests, it does so with accumulated strength, verve, and a visceral rage that is also a form of love, both for those it holds close and for those to follow in potentially changed futures. The lively inventiveness of these poems is part of the work of making space for new ways of thinking and being, for developing 'star-stuffed ears' that might attune us differently to others and to the world."

Zoë Skoulding, *A Marginal Sea*